PRINCEWILL LAGANG

True Love Waits: Christian Dating and Purity

Contents

1

True Love Waits - Christian Dating and Purity

The sun dipped below the horizon, casting a warm, golden hue across the small town of Graceville. It was a picturesque evening, a perfect backdrop for the budding romance between Sarah and Michael. They had been friends for years, brought together by their shared faith and a commitment to living a life that honored God. Both of them believed in the value of purity in their dating relationship, and tonight was the beginning of their journey.

1.1 A Foundation of Faith

The story of Sarah and Michael's love affair is one that explores the deep-seated principles that underpin Christian dating. In a world marked by casual relationships and fleeting connections, their journey would be a testament to the enduring values of faith, purity, and waiting for true love.

Sarah and Michael were firm believers in the power of their Christian faith. For them, it wasn't just a label or a tradition; it was the bedrock upon which they built their lives. They both understood that faith wasn't just a Sunday morning ritual but a way of life, a guide for every aspect of their existence, including dating.

1.2 The Pursuit of Purity

Purity was a concept that held a special place in their hearts. They believed in preserving the sanctity of their bodies and souls, reserving the gift of physical intimacy for the one they would one day call their spouse. In a society that often prioritized instant gratification, they were committed to maintaining the sanctity of their connection. Their choice to abstain from physical intimacy wasn't about repression; it was about honoring each other and, most importantly, honoring God.

1.3 True Love Waits

The phrase "True Love Waits" became their mantra. It reminded them that real love was worth the wait. It encouraged them to be patient in their dating journey, allowing their connection to grow deeper and stronger. They knew that love was not a rush to the finish line but a journey to be savored, step by step.

In the realm of Christian dating, "True Love Waits" is more than just a slogan; it's a commitment to purity and a dedication to seeking God's guidance in the pursuit of a lifelong partnership. It's a promise to each other and to their Creator that they would patiently and faithfully wait for the person God had chosen for them.

1.4 The Purpose of This Book

In the pages that follow, we will explore the beautiful tapestry of Christian dating and purity. This book will delve into the principles, challenges, and rewards of pursuing love in the light of faith. It will offer guidance, stories, and wisdom from both Sarah and Michael, as well as other couples who have walked a similar path.

The journey of Christian dating is an inspiring and often arduous one. In a world that values instant gratification, it stands as a testament to the enduring power of patience, faith, and love. In the chapters ahead, we will explore the foundations of Christian dating, the challenges it presents, and the profound beauty of waiting for true love.

In "True Love Waits: Christian Dating and Purity," we will embark on a journey of the heart and spirit, guided by the principles of faith, purity, and the unwavering belief that true love is indeed worth waiting for.

2

The Foundations of Christian Dating

In Chapter 1, we introduced the concept of "True Love Waits" as the guiding principle for Christian dating and purity. Now, in Chapter 2, we will delve deeper into the foundations of Christian dating, exploring the core values and beliefs that provide the sturdy framework for a relationship that honors God.

2.1 The Biblical Blueprint

For Sarah and Michael, like many other Christian couples, the Bible served as their ultimate guide. The Word of God outlined not only the principles of faith but also the blueprint for a healthy, God-honoring relationship. They turned to passages like 1 Corinthians 6:18-20, which reminds believers that their bodies are temples of the Holy Spirit, and therefore, should be treated with respect and purity.

Ephesians 5:25 was another verse they clung to. It emphasizes the sacrificial love that husbands should have for their wives, mirroring the love of Christ for the Church. This verse set the standard for how Michael would love and honor Sarah in their relationship.

2.2 Prayer and Seeking God's Will

Christian dating is not about following a one-size-fits-all formula. Instead, it's about seeking God's will in every step of the journey. Sarah and Michael understood that prayer was a vital part of their relationship. They sought God's guidance in their decision to date and continued to pray together for His direction.

Their trust in God's guidance extended to every aspect of their lives, from career choices to where they would live. They recognized that God's plan was greater than their own, and they were willing to surrender their desires to His divine purpose.

2.3 Accountability and Community

Accountability played a significant role in their relationship. They sought out mentors and friends who shared their faith and values, individuals who could provide guidance and support. These mentors were trusted advisors who could offer wisdom when challenges arose.

Their community also provided a strong support system. The church they attended became a place of fellowship and encouragement. They attended youth groups and participated in Bible studies, connecting with others who shared their commitment to Christian dating and purity.

2.4 Defining Boundaries

One of the most crucial aspects of Christian dating is setting and respecting boundaries. Sarah and Michael knew the importance of clearly defining their limits and expectations. They communicated openly about physical boundaries, discussing what they were comfortable with and where they needed to exercise caution.

Beyond physical boundaries, they also set emotional and spiritual boundaries. They recognized that it was essential to safeguard their hearts and minds, preserving their emotional purity as well.

2.5 Patience and Trust

Patience is a cornerstone of Christian dating. Sarah and Michael knew that true love couldn't be rushed. They trusted that God had a plan for their relationship and that waiting for the right time was a display of their faith.

Throughout their dating journey, they faced challenges and doubts. Yet, their trust in God's plan and their unwavering commitment to each other carried them through those tough times. They understood that even when the path seemed unclear, they could rely on their faith and each other.

Chapter 2 has explored the foundations of Christian dating: the importance of biblical guidance, the role of prayer and seeking God's will, the necessity of accountability and community, the significance of defining boundaries, and the enduring value of patience and trust. In the chapters to come, we will continue to uncover the principles and practices that make "True Love Waits" a beautiful and fulfilling approach to Christian dating and purity.

3

Building a Strong Foundation

In Chapter 2, we explored the foundations of Christian dating, emphasizing the importance of faith, prayer, boundaries, accountability, and patience. Now, in Chapter 3, we will delve into the process of building a strong foundation for a Christ-centered relationship.

3.1 The Dating Relationship

For Sarah and Michael, their dating relationship was a journey of discovery. It was a period of getting to know each other on a deeper level while aligning their lives with shared values and faith. In Christian dating, the dating phase is an essential time to establish a strong foundation.

3.2 Shared Faith and Values

The core of their relationship was built upon a shared faith and values. They both believed in the fundamental importance of putting God first in their lives. Their faith wasn't just a side note; it was the cornerstone upon which their love was constructed.

Beyond faith, they also shared other values, like honesty, kindness, and humility. They believed in treating others with respect and dignity, which extended to their relationship as well. Their shared values created a strong common ground on which they could build their future.

3.3 Effective Communication

Open and effective communication was another key element in constructing a solid foundation. Sarah and Michael were committed to transparent and honest discussions. They knew that good communication was not just about talking but also about active listening and understanding each other's perspectives.

Effective communication allowed them to address concerns, celebrate achievements, and grow together as a couple. It was a vital tool in resolving conflicts and building a strong, trusting relationship.

3.4 Spiritual Growth Together

In a Christ-centered relationship, spiritual growth is not a solo endeavor. Sarah and Michael believed in growing together in their faith. They attended church services together, read the Bible as a couple, and discussed their spiritual journeys openly.

This shared spiritual growth created a strong bond between them, allowing them to draw closer to God and to each other. It also helped them navigate the challenges that arose in their relationship and provided them with a sense of unity.

3.5 Building Trust

Trust was a crucial element of their foundation. It took time to develop, and they understood that trust wasn't just handed over; it was earned. They worked to maintain honesty, loyalty, and consistency in their relationship.

They were also mindful of their commitments and promises. This trust extended beyond their relationship to their families and communities, demonstrating their reliability and faithfulness.

3.6 Preparing for the Future

While they were building their foundation, Sarah and Michael were also preparing for the future. They discussed their individual goals and dreams, making sure they aligned with their shared values and faith. They believed in the importance of a shared vision for their life together.

As they continued to date, they began to talk about the possibility of marriage and family. They recognized the importance of seeking God's guidance in these significant decisions and knew that their strong foundation would be instrumental in building a lasting marriage.

Chapter 3 has explored the process of building a strong foundation in Christian dating. The key elements include shared faith and values, effective communication, spiritual growth together, building trust, and preparing for the future. In the following chapters, we will delve deeper into the challenges and rewards of "True Love Waits" in the context of Christian dating and purity.

4

Navigating Challenges and Temptations

In the previous chapters, we've examined the foundations and the importance of building a strong Christian relationship. Now, in Chapter 4, we'll explore the challenges and temptations that can arise when following the "True Love Waits" philosophy in Christian dating.

4.1 The Battle of Temptation

Sarah and Michael were no strangers to the temptations that can arise in a dating relationship. Temptation comes in various forms, from physical desires to emotional challenges. It's a test of the commitment to purity and the shared values they hold dear.

Temptations are not something to be ashamed of; they are a natural part of human relationships. What matters is how they are managed and resisted within the context of Christian dating.

4.2 Physical Temptations

One of the primary challenges in Christian dating is managing physical temptations. The desire for physical intimacy is a natural part of any romantic relationship. However, "True Love Waits" requires couples to maintain purity until marriage.

To resist these physical temptations, Sarah and Michael practiced strict boundaries, including refraining from situations that might lead to compromise. They sought the accountability of mentors and trusted friends who could provide guidance during moments of weakness.

4.3 Emotional Temptations

Emotional temptations can be equally challenging. In the course of their relationship, Sarah and Michael occasionally faced jealousy, insecurity, and conflicts that could strain their emotional purity. Their shared faith, open communication, and mutual support helped them navigate these emotions.

They learned to address emotional temptations by acknowledging their feelings, discussing them openly, and seeking God's guidance in resolving conflicts. Emotional purity was preserved by fostering a loving, forgiving, and understanding atmosphere in their relationship.

4.4 Peer Pressure

In a world that often emphasizes instant gratification and casual relationships, Sarah and Michael sometimes felt the pressure to conform to societal norms. They encountered criticism from friends who didn't understand their commitment to Christian dating and purity.

Overcoming peer pressure required a steadfast belief in their values and a clear understanding of their purpose. They relied on their support system of like-minded friends and mentors who encouraged their commitment.

4.5 Maintaining Patience

Another challenge they faced was the impatience that could come with waiting for true love. In a world of quick solutions and immediate satisfaction, they sometimes questioned whether their decision to wait was the right one.

To maintain their patience, they continued to pray, trust in God's plan, and seek comfort in the belief that true love was indeed worth waiting for. Their patience was not passive but an active choice to nurture their relationship at a steady, God-ordained pace.

4.6 God's Grace and Forgiveness

Sarah and Michael knew that they were not perfect, and their relationship wasn't without its mistakes and missteps. But they also understood the profound grace and forgiveness that God offers. They relied on His forgiveness to move forward, using their experiences as opportunities for growth.

Christian dating isn't about perfection; it's about striving to honor God's principles and relying on His grace when mistakes are made. They believed that God's grace was an essential component of their journey.

Chapter 4 has explored the challenges and temptations faced by Christian couples who embrace the "True Love Waits" philosophy. These include physical and emotional temptations, peer pressure, maintaining patience, and the role of God's grace and forgiveness. In the following chapters, we'll continue to explore the rewards and joys that come with navigating these challenges while preserving purity in Christian dating.

5

The Rewards of Faithful Waiting

In Chapter 4, we examined the challenges and temptations that Christian couples may encounter while adhering to the "True Love Waits" philosophy. Now, in Chapter 5, we will explore the rich and lasting rewards that come from faithfully waiting for true love in the context of Christian dating and purity.

5.1 A Deepening Connection

One of the most profound rewards of embracing "True Love Waits" is the deepening connection between partners. By prioritizing emotional and spiritual intimacy over physical intimacy, couples like Sarah and Michael discover a bond that goes beyond the surface. Their love is built on shared values, trust, and a profound understanding of each other's hearts and souls.

This deep connection allows them to build a solid foundation for their future marriage. Their relationship isn't merely physical; it's a true partnership of two individuals who are united in faith and love.

5.2 Emotional Stability

In Christian dating, where boundaries and purity are maintained, couples often experience greater emotional stability. They are less likely to face the rollercoaster of emotions that can come from casual or impulsive relationships. This stability provides a sense of security and peace within the relationship.

Sarah and Michael recognized that, by maintaining emotional purity, they could navigate challenges and conflicts more effectively. Their commitment to open communication and trust contributed to a harmonious and stable partnership.

5.3 A Testimony of Faith

Embracing "True Love Waits" isn't just about a personal journey; it's also a powerful testimony of faith to the world. By living out their values and principles, couples like Sarah and Michael become beacons of light in a world that often prioritizes instant gratification and compromise.

Their relationship becomes a living testament to the enduring power of faith, patience, and trust in God's plan. Others may be inspired and encouraged by their example, perhaps even choosing to follow a similar path.

5.4 The Joy of God's Timing

"True Love Waits" is a belief in God's perfect timing. Christian couples who embrace this philosophy experience the joy of waiting for the right person in God's appointed time. It's an anticipation and excitement that can't be replicated by rushed or hasty relationships.

Sarah and Michael felt that their patient waiting was rewarded with a love that was not only fulfilling but also perfectly timed. They cherished the journey that brought them together and were grateful for God's guidance.

5.5 Preparing for a God-Honoring Marriage

Ultimately, the most significant reward of faithful waiting is the preparation for a God-honoring marriage. By building a relationship on shared faith, trust, open communication, and patience, couples are better equipped to face the challenges and joys of marriage.

Sarah and Michael knew that their commitment to "True Love Waits" had not only brought them to the threshold of marriage but had also equipped them to nurture a lasting, fulfilling, and God-honoring partnership.

Chapter 5 has explored the rewards of faithful waiting in Christian dating and purity, including a deepening connection, emotional stability, a testimony of faith, the joy of God's timing, and preparation for a God-honoring marriage. In the upcoming chapters, we will delve into practical advice and tips for couples who aspire to follow the "True Love Waits" philosophy on their own Christian dating journey.

6

Practical Guidance for "True Love Waits"

In the preceding chapters, we have explored the principles, foundations, challenges, and rewards of "True Love Waits" in Christian dating. In Chapter 6, we will provide practical guidance and advice for couples who are committed to pursuing purity in their dating relationships.

6.1 Establish Clear Boundaries

Setting clear boundaries is essential for maintaining purity in a Christian dating relationship. Sarah and Michael understood the importance of defining their limits early in their relationship. They communicated openly about their expectations regarding physical, emotional, and spiritual boundaries.

When establishing boundaries, it's crucial to be specific. Clearly define what actions are off-limits and discuss what activities are acceptable. It's also important to revisit and adjust boundaries as the relationship evolves and matures.

6.2 Engage in Accountability

Accountability is a powerful tool in upholding purity in Christian dating. Seek out mentors, friends, or couples who can provide guidance and support.

Share your boundaries with them and allow them to hold you accountable.

For Sarah and Michael, their accountability partners played a pivotal role in helping them resist temptation and navigate challenges. Regular check-ins and open conversations helped keep their relationship on the path of purity.

6.3 Prioritize Spiritual Growth

A strong focus on spiritual growth is central to "True Love Waits." Attend church services together, engage in Bible study, and pray as a couple. These practices will not only deepen your faith but also provide a spiritual anchor for your relationship.

Spiritual growth helps you stay connected to God and each other. It fosters a sense of unity and purpose that is invaluable in maintaining purity in your relationship.

6.4 Foster Open Communication

Open and honest communication is the lifeblood of a successful Christian dating relationship. Address concerns, challenges, and emotions as they arise. Discuss your desires, expectations, and doubts openly with your partner.

Sarah and Michael valued their ability to talk about everything, even when it was difficult. They knew that open communication helped them maintain emotional purity and navigate the trials they encountered.

6.5 Seek God's Guidance

As you navigate your Christian dating journey, continue to seek God's guidance. Trust that He has a plan for your relationship. Pray individually and as a couple, asking for His wisdom and strength.

Sarah and Michael's unwavering trust in God's plan was a cornerstone of their relationship. They relied on Him for direction and found peace in His guidance.

6.6 Practice Patience

Patience is key in "True Love Waits." Remember that love is worth the wait. Avoid rushing into physical intimacy or making impulsive decisions. Trust that God's timing is perfect.

Sarah and Michael considered their patient waiting to be a testament to their faith and love. They knew that their patience was a virtue that would be rewarded in the end.

Chapter 6 has provided practical guidance for couples who aspire to follow the "True Love Waits" philosophy in Christian dating. By establishing clear boundaries, engaging in accountability, prioritizing spiritual growth, fostering open communication, seeking God's guidance, and practicing patience, you can navigate the challenges of purity in your relationship while reaping the lasting rewards of faith and love. In the upcoming chapters, we will explore real-life stories and experiences from other Christian couples who have embraced "True Love Waits."

7

Real-Life Stories of "True Love Waits"

In this chapter, we will delve into the real-life experiences of Christian couples who have embraced the "True Love Waits" philosophy in their dating relationships. These stories provide valuable insights and inspiration for those on a similar journey, highlighting the challenges, rewards, and unique paths each couple has taken.

7.1 Sarah and Michael: A Testimony of Love and Faith

Sarah and Michael's journey, which we've followed throughout this book, serves as a remarkable testament to the power of "True Love Waits." Their story underscores the enduring strength of a relationship founded on shared faith, clear boundaries, open communication, and unwavering patience. As they prepare to enter the sacred bond of marriage, they stand as an example of a couple who have truly waited for true love.

7.2 Emily and Daniel: A Story of Redemption

Emily and Daniel's story is one of redemption and second chances. They both came from backgrounds of brokenness and had made mistakes in their past. When they met, they felt God's call to pursue a path of purity and holiness. Their journey has been marked by healing, forgiveness, and the restoration of their faith. Through "True Love Waits," they found a love that is truly transformative.

7.3 Rebecca and John: A Long-Distance Love

Rebecca and John's relationship started as a long-distance love story. The physical separation posed a unique challenge, but they saw it as an opportunity to prioritize emotional and spiritual intimacy. Their commitment to open communication, prayer, and shared spiritual growth kept their connection strong. They found that "True Love Waits" transcended distance and time.

7.4 Grace and Samuel: A Journey of Discovery

Grace and Samuel embarked on their Christian dating journey with the belief that they were embarking on a journey of discovery. Their relationship has been marked by curiosity, exploration, and a genuine desire to know each other's hearts and minds. They've learned that love isn't just about waiting; it's about actively getting to know one another while preserving purity.

7.5 Olivia and Ethan: A Path of Faith and Friendship

Olivia and Ethan's relationship began with a strong foundation of friendship. They understood that friendship is a crucial component of love. As they transitioned into dating, they continued to prioritize their deep connection, combining faith, trust, and open communication. Their journey demonstrates that the transition from friendship to romance can be a beautiful one when guided by "True Love Waits."

These real-life stories offer a glimpse into the diversity of experiences within Christian dating relationships that adhere to "True Love Waits." While each journey is unique, they all share a common thread of faith, patience, and a commitment to preserving purity until the right time. The lessons learned from these couples can provide guidance, inspiration, and encouragement for those who aspire to follow a similar path in their own relationships.

21

8

Celebrating "True Love Waits"

In this final chapter of our exploration of "True Love Waits" in Christian dating and purity, we will celebrate the profound beauty and significance of this philosophy. We will reflect on the enduring values it represents, the impact it has on individuals and couples, and the hope it offers for lasting love and spiritual fulfillment.

8.1 The Enduring Values of "True Love Waits"

"True Love Waits" is more than just a phrase; it encapsulates a set of enduring values deeply rooted in faith and love. It signifies the importance of purity, patience, and trust in a world where instant gratification often takes precedence. It underscores the significance of preserving the sanctity of physical and emotional intimacy, prioritizing faith, and actively seeking God's guidance in the realm of romance. These values stand as a counter-cultural declaration, a testament to the enduring principles of a faith-based relationship.

8.2 Impact on Individuals and Couples

The impact of "True Love Waits" on individuals and couples is profound. It promotes self-control, self-respect, and the preservation of emotional and physical purity. It strengthens communication, trust, and shared values within a relationship. Couples who embrace this philosophy often find that their love is deeper and more meaningful, grounded in a foundation of faith and mutual respect.

For individuals, it offers a path to personal growth and a deeper connection with God. It teaches patience, resilience, and the ability to discern God's will in matters of the heart. It encourages individuals to develop a sense of self-worth that is not defined by physical intimacy but by their identity as a child of God.

8.3 The Hope for Lasting Love

"True Love Waits" offers the hope of lasting love. By prioritizing faith, purity, and patience, it paves the way for a love that is not only built to last but also deeply fulfilling. Couples who embrace this philosophy embark on a journey towards a Christ-centered marriage that can withstand the tests of time and trials.

In a world where many relationships are fleeting, marked by heartbreak and disappointment, "True Love Waits" provides hope for a different kind of love – one that is based on faith, trust, and a commitment to God's plan. It is a love worth waiting for, a love that endures, and a love that leads to a joyous and fulfilling marriage.

8.4 A Call to Embrace "True Love Waits"

As we conclude our exploration of "True Love Waits," we extend a call to embrace this philosophy in your own Christian dating journey. Whether you are just beginning to date or have been in a relationship for some time, "True Love Waits" offers a profound and transformative path to love, faith, and fulfillment.

It's a call to prioritize purity, patience, and faith, to resist the temptations of a hurried world, and to wait for the love that God has planned for you. "True Love Waits" is an affirmation that, in the end, true love is worth the wait, and the journey towards it is a beautiful and faith-filled one.

In the pages of this book, we have explored the principles, foundations, challenges, rewards, real-life stories, and celebration of "True Love Waits" in Christian dating and purity. As you embark on your own journey, may you find inspiration and guidance to make "True Love Waits" a foundational philosophy in your life and relationships.

9

Embracing "True Love Waits" in Your Own Journey

In this final chapter of our book on "True Love Waits" in Christian dating and purity, we will provide practical steps and advice for individuals and couples looking to embrace this philosophy in their own relationship journey. This chapter aims to offer guidance and encouragement for those who wish to make "True Love Waits" a foundational principle in their lives.

9.1 Reflect on Your Values

Before embarking on your Christian dating journey, take time to reflect on your values and beliefs. What does your faith mean to you, and how do you want it to shape your relationships? Understand the significance of purity, patience, and trust in your faith.

Consider creating a list of values and principles that are important to you and discuss them with your potential partner. Being clear about your values will help guide your decisions and actions in your dating relationship.

9.2 Set Clear Boundaries

Establishing clear boundaries is essential. Define your physical, emotional, and spiritual boundaries. Discuss these boundaries with your partner and ensure that you both have a shared understanding of what is acceptable and what is not.

Remember that setting boundaries is not about repression but about preserving purity and honoring your faith. Your boundaries are a reflection of your commitment to "True Love Waits."

9.3 Seek Accountability

Accountability is a powerful tool in maintaining purity in your Christian dating relationship. Find mentors, friends, or couples who can provide guidance, support, and accountability. Share your boundaries with them and allow them to help you stay on track.

Having someone to confide in, who shares your values and can offer guidance, is invaluable in navigating the challenges that may arise in your relationship.

9.4 Prioritize Spiritual Growth

Make spiritual growth a central focus of your relationship. Attend church services together, engage in Bible study, and pray as a couple. These practices will help you stay connected to God and each other.

Spiritual growth fosters a deep bond and unity between you and your partner. It provides a strong foundation on which to build your relationship and maintain purity.

9.5 Communicate Openly

Open and honest communication is crucial in preserving emotional purity and resolving conflicts. Be willing to address concerns, share your emotions, and discuss your desires and expectations.

Foster an atmosphere of trust and understanding in your relationship. Make sure you and your partner are comfortable talking about anything and everything that matters to you.

9.6 Trust God's Plan

Throughout your Christian dating journey, continue to trust in God's plan. Seek His guidance through prayer and maintain faith that His timing is perfect. Remember that "True Love Waits" is a declaration of your trust in His purpose for your life.

Embrace the journey, be patient, and let your faith be your guiding light in your pursuit of a Christ-centered, fulfilling relationship.

In Conclusion

"True Love Waits" is not just a philosophy; it's a way of life. It's a commitment to preserving purity, patience, and faith in the realm of Christian dating. Embracing this philosophy in your own journey can lead to a love that is deep, lasting, and centered on God.

As you embark on your Christian dating journey, remember that "True Love Waits" is a path filled with challenges and rewards. It's an affirmation that true love is worth waiting for, and the journey is a beautiful one filled with faith, trust, and the fulfillment of God's plan.

10

A Future of Love and Faith

In this final chapter of "True Love Waits: Christian Dating and Purity," we look to the future and consider the lifelong impact of embracing this philosophy in your Christian dating journey. It's an opportunity to reflect on the enduring values, lessons learned, and the potential for a love-filled future grounded in faith.

10.1 A Love That Lasts a Lifetime

The journey of "True Love Waits" is not confined to your dating years; it's a philosophy that extends to marriage and beyond. When you preserve purity and maintain faith throughout your dating relationship, you are sowing the seeds for a love that lasts a lifetime.

Your commitment to purity, patience, and faith continues to bear fruit throughout your married life. It strengthens your bond as a couple and fosters a love that deepens with time. "True Love Waits" is a philosophy that sets the stage for a lasting, fulfilling, and God-honoring marriage.

10.2 A Testament to Your Faith

Your decision to embrace "True Love Waits" serves as a powerful testament to your faith. It stands as a living example of the values and principles you hold dear. This testimony can inspire and encourage others, whether they are on a similar journey or seeking a deeper connection with their faith.

As you move forward in your relationship, remember the impact you can have on those around you. Your faith, patience, and unwavering commitment to purity are a beacon of light in a world that often values instant gratification and compromise.

10.3 Navigating the Challenges of Marriage

Marriage is a journey filled with its own set of challenges, but the lessons learned in "True Love Waits" can serve as valuable tools. The open communication, trust, and shared values that you've cultivated in your dating relationship will continue to be essential in your marriage.

In your married life, continue to prioritize your faith and the principles that have guided your journey. Be prepared to face the challenges that may arise, and rely on the enduring strength of your "True Love Waits" philosophy to navigate them with grace and unity.

10.4 A Legacy of Love

As you move forward in your journey, consider the legacy you are creating. The values and principles you've embraced will shape not only your own life but also the lives of your future family. Your commitment to purity, patience, and faith can become a legacy that impacts generations to come.

Let your love be an enduring testimony, a testament to the beauty of a faith-based relationship that endures. Consider how your choices today will influence the love and faith of those who follow in your footsteps.

In Conclusion

"True Love Waits" is not just a philosophy; it's a way of life that extends far beyond the dating years. It's a commitment to preserving purity, patience, and faith in every aspect of your relationship, whether in dating, marriage, or family life.

As you look toward the future, remember that the values and principles of "True Love Waits" are timeless. They will continue to guide your journey, strengthen your bond, and serve as a testament to your faith. In your love-filled future, "True Love Waits" remains a foundational philosophy that endures and flourishes.

11

Your Personal Journey with "True Love Waits"

In this concluding chapter, we explore your personal journey with "True Love Waits" in Christian dating and purity. This chapter is dedicated to helping you reflect on your experiences, embrace the principles that resonate with you, and consider how you can apply them to your own life and relationships.

11.1 Reflect on Your Past

Start your journey with introspection. Reflect on your past dating experiences, if any, and the lessons you've learned along the way. What have been your challenges, successes, and moments of growth? Your past experiences can be valuable sources of insight.

Take time to consider your values, beliefs, and how your faith shapes your outlook on love and relationships. Understanding your past and present will help you make informed choices moving forward.

11.2 Clarify Your Relationship Goals

What are your relationship goals and aspirations? Are you seeking a committed, long-term relationship leading to marriage, or are you exploring dating for personal growth and self-discovery? Clarifying your goals is essential to finding alignment with the principles of "True Love Waits."

Consider whether you are looking for someone who shares your faith and values, or if you are open to helping someone grow in their own faith journey. Having a clear vision of your relationship goals will guide your actions and decisions.

11.3 Set Boundaries and Expectations

Once you've clarified your goals, it's time to set boundaries and expectations for your future relationships. What are your non-negotiables when it comes to faith, values, and purity? Define your boundaries for physical, emotional, and spiritual intimacy.

Communicate these boundaries with potential partners and be willing to discuss them openly. Having well-defined boundaries helps create a healthy and respectful foundation for your relationships.

11.4 Build a Support System

Just as Sarah and Michael had mentors and friends to provide accountability and guidance, consider building a support system for your journey. Seek out individuals who share your faith and values and can offer wisdom and encouragement.

Your support system can include mentors, trusted friends, and a church community. They can provide valuable insights, be a source of accountability, and offer emotional support when you face challenges.

11.5 Prioritize Open Communication

Open and honest communication is vital to a successful relationship. Make an effort to cultivate a habit of transparent communication with your partner. Discuss your desires, concerns, and any conflicts that arise.

Active listening and understanding your partner's perspective are equally important. Effective communication fosters trust and helps maintain emotional purity.

11.6 Trust in God's Plan

Finally, trust in God's plan for your life. Embrace patience and faith as you navigate your Christian dating journey. Remember that "True Love Waits" is not just about waiting for love; it's about actively seeking God's will and trusting His timing.

Even when you face uncertainties or challenges, trust that God has a purpose for your journey. Continue to seek His guidance through prayer, knowing that His plan is greater than your own.

In Conclusion

Your personal journey with "True Love Waits" in Christian dating and purity is a unique and transformative experience. It's a path that allows you to align your relationships with your faith, values, and commitment to purity. By reflecting on your past, clarifying your goals, setting boundaries, building a support system, prioritizing open communication, and trusting in God's plan, you can embark on a journey that leads to a lasting, God-honoring love.

12

Conclusion - The Eternal Impact of "True Love Waits"

As we conclude our exploration of "True Love Waits" in Christian dating and purity, let us reflect on the enduring impact this philosophy can have on your life, relationships, and faith. The principles of purity, patience, and faith are not just concepts; they are the building blocks of a love story that can span a lifetime.

12.1 The Ripple Effect of "True Love Waits"

The choices you make in your Christian dating journey, grounded in the principles of "True Love Waits," can create a ripple effect that touches the lives of those around you. Your commitment to faith, purity, and patience becomes a testimony that inspires and encourages others on their own journey.

As you live out these principles, you become a beacon of hope and a living example of the beauty of a faith-based relationship. The impact of "True Love Waits" extends far beyond your own story, creating positive change in the lives of others.

12.2 Embracing God's Plan

"True Love Waits" is not just about waiting for love; it's about embracing God's plan for your life. It's a declaration of your trust in His timing and His purpose. As you continue your journey, remember that God's plan for your life is greater than anything you could ever imagine.

Trust in His wisdom and guidance, knowing that He is leading you toward a love story that is tailor-made for you. "True Love Waits" is a celebration of His plan, a path of faith, and an affirmation of His perfect timing.

12.3 A Love That Lasts

By embracing "True Love Waits," you are not only preserving purity and patience; you are also setting the stage for a love that lasts a lifetime. The enduring values of faith, trust, and commitment to God's plan become the bedrock of your love story.

As you move forward in your relationships, remember that your journey is not defined solely by the waiting, but by the love that is nurtured, deepened, and sustained through the journey. "True Love Waits" is a commitment to a love that stands the test of time and continues to grow in beauty and depth.

12.4 Your Ongoing Journey

Your journey with "True Love Waits" does not end with this book; it continues to evolve and unfold as you live out its principles. As you navigate the challenges, joys, and lessons that come your way, may you find strength in your faith and trust in God's plan.

Remember that your story is unique, and the impact you have on the world, no matter how small or grand, is significant. Embrace the values of purity, patience, and faith, and let them guide you as you create a love story that is a testament to your faith and a reflection of God's grace.

In Conclusion

"True Love Waits" is not just a philosophy; it's a way of life, a declaration of faith, and a commitment to a love story that endures. It's a celebration of the enduring values of purity, patience, and trust in God's plan. May your journey be marked by the profound impact of these principles, and may your love story be a shining example of the beauty of a faith-based relationship.

Book Summary: "True Love Waits: Christian Dating and Purity"

"True Love Waits: Christian Dating and Purity" is a compelling journey into the world of faith-based relationships, focusing on the principles of purity, patience, and faith in the context of Christian dating. This book explores the timeless values that underpin "True Love Waits" and offers practical guidance, real-life stories, and inspiration for individuals and couples seeking to embrace this philosophy in their own journey.

The book unfolds in twelve chapters, each with a unique focus:

1. Foundation of Faith: This chapter sets the stage by introducing the core principles of "True Love Waits," emphasizing the importance of faith, trust, and God's plan in Christian dating.

2. The Beauty of Purity: It explores the significance of preserving physical and emotional purity in relationships and the impact of these choices on personal growth and faith.

3. Embracing Patience: This chapter delves into the value of patience and how it paves the way for a love story that unfolds in God's perfect time.

4. Nurturing Faith: It underscores the role of faith as the cornerstone of Christian dating, emphasizing the importance of shared values and spiritual growth.

5. Starting the Journey: Practical advice is offered for individuals and couples looking to begin their Christian dating journey with the principles of "True Love Waits."

6. Developing Emotional Intimacy: The book explores the significance of emotional intimacy and how it can deepen the connection in faith-based relationships.

7. Maintaining Physical Purity: This chapter provides guidance on managing physical temptations, setting boundaries, and preserving purity until marriage.

8. Navigating Challenges and Temptations: It delves into the common challenges faced by Christian couples in adhering to "True Love Waits," such as peer pressure, emotional temptations, and maintaining patience.

9. The Rewards of Faithful Waiting: The chapter explores the rewards that come from embracing "True Love Waits," including deepening connections, emotional stability, and a testimony of faith to the world.

10. Practical Guidance for "True Love Waits": It offers practical steps and advice for individuals and couples who aspire to follow the philosophy in their own dating relationships, including setting clear boundaries, seeking accountability, and fostering open communication.

11. Real-Life Stories of "True Love Waits": The book shares the real-life experiences of Christian couples who have embraced "True Love Waits" in their dating journeys, offering valuable insights and inspiration.

12. Your Personal Journey with "True Love Waits": The final chapter focuses on your own personal journey with "True Love Waits," offering guidance on setting boundaries, building a support system, and trusting in God's plan.

The book concludes by highlighting the eternal impact of "True Love Waits," emphasizing the ripple effect on others, the significance of embracing God's plan, and the potential for a love that lasts a lifetime.

"True Love Waits: Christian Dating and Purity" is a comprehensive guide that combines faith, values, and practical advice to help individuals and couples create fulfilling, God-honoring relationships. It inspires readers to navigate the challenges of dating with patience and purity, ultimately leading to a love story that stands the test of time.